POETRY Alive!

Leslie Feierstone Barna

Acknowledgments

The publisher gratefully acknowledges permission to reprint
the following copyrighted material.

"April Rain Song" from THE DREAM KEEPER AND OTHER POEMS by Langston Hughes.
Copyright © 1932 by Alfred A. Knopf, Inc. and renewed 1960 by Langston Hughes. Reprinted by
permission of the publisher. Australian rights administered by Harold Ober Associates, Inc.

"Brother": reprinted by permission of Gina Maccoby Literary Agency © 1959. Renewed 1987 by
Mary Ann Hoberman.

"Desert Tortoise": reprinted by permission of Charles Scribner's Sons, an imprint of Macmillan
Publishing Company, from DESERT VOICES by Byrd Baylor. Copyright © 1981 by Byrd Baylor.

"Home! You're Where It's Warm Inside" by Jack Prelutsky from THE RANDOM HOUSE
BOOK OF POETRY FOR CHILDREN, selected and introduced by Jack Prelutsky. Copyright
© 1983 by Jack Prelutsky. Reprinted by permission of Random House, Inc.

"Life In The Forest. Or: Bad News . . . Good News . . . Bad News. . . ." from CHOCOLATE
DREAMS by Arnold Adoff, illustrated by Turi MacCombie, published by Lothrop, Lee &
Shepard Books, a division of William Morrow and Company, Inc./Publishers, New York, 1989.
Text copyright © 1989 by Arnold Adoff. Illustrations copyright © 1989 by Turi MacCombie.
Reprinted by permission of William Morrow and Company, Inc./Publishers, New York.

"The Man in the Onion Bed" from I MET A MAN by John Ciardi. Copyright © 1961 by John
Ciardi. Reprinted by permission of Houghton Mifflin Company. All rights reserved.

"My Four Friends" from ROLLING HARVEY DOWN THE HILL by Jack Prelutsky, illustrated
by Victoria Chess, published by Greenwillow Books, a division of William Morrow and
Company, Inc./Publishers, New York, 1980. Text copyright © 1980 by Jack Prelutsky.
Illustrations copyright © 1980 by Victoria Chess. Reprinted by permission of William Morrow
and Company, Inc./Publishers, New York.

"The Spangled Pandemonium" from BEYOND THE PAW PAW TREES by Palmer Brown.
Copyright © 1954 by Palmer Brown. Reprinted by permission of HarperCollins Publishers.

"Tree House" from WHERE THE SIDEWALK ENDS by Shel Silverstein. Copyright © 1974 by
Evil Eye Music, Inc. Selection reprinted by permission of HarperCollins Publishers and Jonathan
Cape. Australian rights administered by Random Century Group.

"Two People" from A WORD OR TWO WITH YOU by Eve Merriam. Copyright © 1981 by Eve
Merriam. Reprinted by permission of Marian Reiner for the author.

"Who Am I?" from AT THE TOP OF MY VOICE AND OTHER POEMS by Felice Holman,
published by Charles Scribner's Sons, 1970. Copyright © 1970 by Felice Holman. Reprinted by
permission of the author and Charles Scribner's Sons.

CONTENTS

Poetry Alive!
Breathing Life into Poetry

Teachers can foster in children a lasting love for poetry. **Poetry Alive!** is meant to help teachers of grades K through 6 create appreciation and excitement for poetry in young readers. A wide variety of poems is included, ranging from the cozy, familiar atmosphere of nursery rhymes and folk songs to contemporary poetry.

Poetry can appeal to children of any age in any grade. It can interest and excite the most talented as well as the most reluctant reader. It can open a world of feelings and responses from children.

The activities in **Poetry Alive!** encourage children to respond to poetry and express themselves through choral reading, drama, singing, art, melody writing, and—of course—poetry writing. Many activities encourage students to consider poems' subjects, initiating explorations of topics covered in a variety of curriculum areas.

The poetry in this book is divided into five thematic units, covering five areas that relate to children's interests. They are entitled "Frolic & Fancy," "Tasty Treats," "Family & Friends," "Featuring Creatures," and "Earth, Sea, & Sky." Preceding the poetry in each unit is a brief introduction and a related bibliography.

Using
Poetry Alive!

The poetry in **Poetry Alive!** is meant to be read to children and by children. Introduce children to a poem either by printing it on the chalkboard or making copies, so that they can read along as you read aloud to familiarize them with rhythmic cadences, content, and rhyme schemes. It is recommended that you read a poem several times to yourself before sharing it with children. The more familiar you are with a poem, the more cadence and drama the children will hear as you read aloud to them. Most of all, take pleasure in the poetry you share! Your enjoyment will certainly be obvious to your listeners.

Following each thematic grouping of poetry and classroom activities are several Activity Sheets. Suggested uses for these Activity Sheets are keyed into the classroom activities; however, you may prefer to have children complete them independently or as a follow-up to the activities.

F r o l i c   &   F a n c y

Childhood is a magical time. Children are free to reflect on themselves and the world around them, and to imagine wonderful creatures and adventures. The magic of childhood is remembered in the selections in "Frolic & Fancy." These poems will take children from imagining what they would do if they were in charge of the world to wondering about how they fit into life's grand scheme. They will imagine fanciful and funny monsters and recall the exhilaration of swinging on a swing. A nonsense song about creatures that do ridiculous things will inspire them to sing along and make up their own silly verses. Limericks will amuse them and they might find the inspiration to write their own.

Step into the world of childhood and encourage children to think about the lighter side of life in new ways.

W h e r e   t o   F i n d   M o r e   P o e m s

Bennett, Jill, ed. **Spooky Poems.** Joy Street, 1989.

cummings, e. e. **hist whist.** Crown, 1989.

Merriam, Eve. **Chortles.** Morrow, 1989.

Yolen, Jane. **Best Witches: Poems for Halloween.** Putnam, 1989.

F r o l i c & F a n c y

Tree House

A tree house, a free house,
A secret you and me house,
A high up in the leafy branches
Cozy as can be house.

A street house, a neat house,
Be sure and wipe your feet house
Is not my kind of house at all—
Let's go live in a tree house.

Shel Silverstein

What I'd Do

If I were the King
    Of Kalamazone,
I'd smile and I'd laugh
    As I sat on my throne.

If I were the King
    Of Kalamazin,
I'd perch on my throne
    With a big, broad grin.

But I am a child
    In Kalamazoo.
So what do you think
    That I mostly do?

I sit on my steps—
    For my throne is wood—
And I chuckle and laugh
    Like a great king should.

Lee Blair

Frolic & Fancy

Comparing Poems

Tell your class that you are going to read two poems in which the speakers dream about what they would do if they were "in charge." Read aloud "Tree House" and "What I'd Do." Discuss with children what each speaker imagines. The speaker in Shel Silverstein's poem wishes he or she could live in a tree house instead of a conventional house where rules and regulations have to be followed. The speaker in Lee Blair's poem would be a merry king on a throne.

Invite children to compare the way each speaker imagines. You might wish to point out that both speakers come back to the real world at points in the poems.

If I Could Have My Way...

Invite children to imagine that they could have their way for a day. Ask them to think about what they would do, who they would be, where they would go, and so on. Encourage them to put their thoughts in the form of a poem. Suggest that children follow a rhyme pattern as in Silverstein's poem or Blair's poem if they wish, and point out that the poems can be any length. When they have finished, invite them to read their poems aloud.

Next, have children work in small groups. Invite each child to organize and direct the others in the group to dramatize his or her poem. Provide a variety of art materials and offer each child the opportunity to make a prop to use while dramatizing his or her poem. Encourage the child to direct other members of the group to act out the parts of inanimate objects as necessary.

Allow groups plenty of time to rehearse. Let each child have a turn as director, and have the groups present their dramatizations to the rest of the class.

Frolic & Fancy

Who Am I?

The trees ask me,
And the sky,
And the sea asks me
  Who am I?

The grass asks me,
And the sand,
And the rocks ask me
  Who I am.

The wind tells me
At nightfall,
And the rain tells me
  Someone small.

  Someone small
  Someone small
  But a piece
    of
      it
      all.

  Felice Holman

NAME POEMS

L   lively
I   interesting
N   nimble
D   decisive
A   athletic

T   terrific
O   open
B   beautiful
Y   young

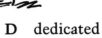

D   dedicated
E   eager
N   neat
N   nice
I   intelligent
S   special

Frolic & Fancy

Writing a Poem About ME

Print the poem "Who Am I?" on the chalkboard or provide children with their own copies, and read it aloud. Call on volunteers to take turns reading the verses. Begin a discussion by asking the following questions:

- Who is the narrator of the poem?
- What question is the narrator being asked?
- Who gives the narrator an answer?
- What answer do they give? Why do you think this might be their answer?

Encourage children to think about how they would answer the question, "Who Am I?" Invite them to write a poem that answers this question. Point out the rhyme scheme in "Who Am I?" Explain that in their poems, they may use any kind of rhyme scheme or none.

Word Portraits

Point out to children that their names tell others who they are. We can say that a name is one small way of describing a person. Invite children to think of some adjectives to create word portraits of themselves. Try to get them to think of several adjectives that describe facets of their personalities. Suggest that they think about things they like to do, special or unique abilities they have, what they like to think about, how they look, how they like to dress, and so on. Ask children to make lists of words that describe them.

Next, print the name poems from page 10 on the chalkboard. Read the descriptors for each letter in the names. Then invite children to write their own name poems using descriptive words from their lists. If they wish, they can write a name poem for both their first and last names. If children need help with descriptors, let them use the thesaurus, books, or magazines for word ideas.

Provide lightweight cardboard. Have children trace and cut out large capital letters, one for each letter in their first names. They can then color the letters and write a descriptor on each letter to create their name poems. Display the finished poems on a bulletin board entitled "Who We Are."

Frolic & Fancy

Fooba Wooba John

Saw a flea kick a tree,
Fooba wooba, fooba wooba,
Saw a flea kick a tree,
Fooba wooba John.
Saw a flea kick a tree
In the middle of the sea,
Fooba wooba, fooba wooba,
Fooba wooba John.

Saw a crow flying low,
Fooba wooba, fooba wooba,
Saw a crow flying low,
Fooba wooba John.
Saw a crow flying low
Several miles beneath the snow,
Fooba wooba, fooba wooba,
Fooba wooba John.

Saw a bug give a shrug . . .
In the middle of the rug . . .

Saw a whale chase a snail . . .
All around a water pail . . .

Saw two geese making cheese . . .
One would hold and the other would squeeze . . .

Saw a mule teaching school . . .
To some bullfrogs in the pool . . .

Saw a bee off to sea . . .
With a fiddle across his knee . . .

Saw a hare chase a deer . . .
Ran it all of seven year . . .

Saw a bear scratch his ear . . .
Wonderin' what we're doing here . . .

American Folk Song

12

Frolic & Fancy

Choral Reading

Read "Fooba Wooba John" aloud several times until children become familiar with the cadence, the rhyme pattern, and the nonsense. Print the poem on the chalkboard or make a copy for each student, and invite them first to read the poem silently and then to read aloud with you. Ask your class if the rhythm of the poem suggests any particular form of movement such as clapping, marching, or moving their bodies in another way. Have children read the poem again, using volunteers' suggestions.

Putting Words to Music

Point out to children that "Fooba Wooba John" is an American folk song. Invite them to work in small groups to try to put the words of the poem to music. Encourage them to think of melodies with which they are familiar and see if the rhythm of the words matches the rhythm of the music, or let them invent a melody of their own. Once they have agreed on a melody, allow them time to practice singing the song. Then invite the groups to sing their versions of "Fooba Wooba John" for the rest of the class.

Adding Verses

Point out the additional verses of "Fooba Wooba John." Ask your class to clap out the rhythm of these lines. Have children write two or three verses that could be added to the song. Children can incorporate these verses into the songs they created in the previous activity.

Drawing a Verse

Provide each child with three or four sheets of drawing paper. Invite children to copy the first two long stanzas of the poem, one to a sheet of paper. Then ask them to write their original two-line verses in place of the existing ones, each on a separate sheet of paper. Children can illustrate each page using crayons, paints, or markers. Next, provide each child with a sheet of construction paper and invite children to make a cover for their poems. Attach the poem pages to the cover sheet and have children share their work with the rest of the group. Display the poetry booklets on a wall or bulletin board for everyone to share.

Frolic & Fancy

The Spangled Pandemonium

The Spangled Pandemonium
Is missing from the zoo.
He bent the bars the barest bit,
And slithered glibly through.

He crawled across the moated wall,
He climbed the mango tree,
And when his keeper scrambled up,
He nipped him in the knee.

To all of you, a warning
Not to wander after dark,
Or if you must, make very sure
You stay out of the park.

For the Spangled Pandemonium
Is missing from the zoo,
And since he nipped his keeper,
He would just as soon nip you!

Palmer Brown

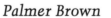

Monsters, Monsters, and More Monsters

Read ''The Spangled Pandemonium'' aloud. Help children to understand the humor. Begin a group discussion about the creature in the poem. Ask children to speculate about how it looks, how it sounds, and special things it does.

Ask children to think about how they would draw this creature, or a monster of their own creation. Then invite them to work in groups of four or five. Provide each group with a sheet of mural paper, crayons, paints, chalk, markers, paste, scraps of fabric and paper, and any other art materials that are handy. Encourage group members to work together to create a monster. Ask them to decide on who will create the head, the body, the arms and legs, a tail, and so on. When the murals are finished, have the groups name their monsters and display them for the rest of the class. Ask a volunteer from each group to share with the class what kind of monster the group created, what it does, where it lives, and how it sounds.

Writing About Monsters

Invite your class to write descriptions of their monsters. On the chalkboard, write the following headings: *Monsters Look Like, Monsters Move, Monsters Sound Like, Monsters Eat, Monsters Live In, Monsters Do, Monsters Don't Like,* and *Monsters Do Like*. Have children list phrases, words, and sentences that fit in each category based on the monster murals.

Writing a Poem About Monsters

Distribute a copy of the Monster Description Sheet (page 22) to each child. Allow children time to complete the Activity Sheet. Then invite them to use the information from the Activity Sheet to write a poem about monsters on another piece of paper. Assist them in creating their poems by asking them to look for a group of words or a sentence that would make a good first line. Do the same for deciding on an appropriate last line. Then ask children to use the rest of their work to write the body of the poem. Finally, ask them to think of a catchy title. Children can illustrate their poems.

When the poems are finished, invite children to share them with the rest of the class. Mount the poems around the monsters on the murals.

Frolic & Fancy

RIDDLES

There is one that has a head without
  an eye,
And there's one that has an eye
  without a head:
You may find the answer if you try;
  And when all is said
Half the answer hangs upon a thread!
                [a needle and thread]

Christina Rossetti

Thirty white horses upon a red hill,
Now they tramp, now they champ,
  now they stand still.

                    [teeth]

Mother Goose

First they dress in green,
  Then they change to brown;
And some will even wear
  A red or golden gown!
                [leaves]

Anonymous

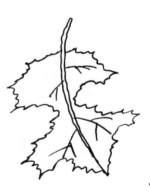

Riddle me, riddle me, what is that,
Over the head, and under the hat?
                [hair]

Anonymous

First it a was pretty flower, dressed
  in pink and white,
Then it was a tiny ball, almost hid
  from sight.
Round and green and large it grew—
  then it turned to red.
It will make a splendid pie for your
  Thanksgiving spread.

                [an apple]

Anonymous

Frolic & Fancy

Look, Taste, Feel, and Smell

Display several apples in class. Explain to children that you want them to describe an apple using single words and phrases. Allow them all to handle an apple. Suggest that they touch, sniff, and look closely at the apple. Cut the apples into several sections and allow children to taste them. Then help children make lists of descriptive words and phrases. First, have children offer words that describe how the apple looks and list them under the heading *The Apple Looks . . . .* Next, ask for words that describe how the apple feels and write them under the heading *The Apple Feels . . . .* Make a third list describing how the apple smells and tastes. Finally, ask children to suggest places where apples can be found and where they like to be when they eat apples.

Riddle Me

Ask children if they can explain what a riddle is. If necessary, tell them that in a riddle, an object is described but not named. Read the riddles on page 16 and let students guess what objects are being described.

Distribute a copy of the Riddle Activity Sheet on page 23 to each child. Direct your class's attention to the lists on the chalkboard that were generated for the activity above. Then have children begin the Activity Sheet by filling in the blanks in line 1 with words from the first list. Ask them to fill in the blanks in line 2 with a phrase from the second list. Next, have them choose words from list 3 to fill in the blanks on the third line. For the fourth and fifth lines, have them choose places from the last list. When children have finished the sheet, encourage them to use their work to write a riddle. Point out that they may use any kind of rhyme scheme or none at all.

An Apple a Day

Have each child cut an apple shape from red construction paper. Have them copy their riddles onto the apple cutout. With brown markers or construction paper, draw or cut out a tree for the bulletin board. Display children's apple riddles by fastening them to the tree limbs.

I am round
And green, yellow, or red.
I feel smooth and firm.
I smell sweet and taste tangy.
You can find me on certain trees

Or in the supermarket.
You can eat me
Anytime you want
A nutritious snack.
What am I ?

Frolic & Fancy

The Swing

How do you like to go up in a swing,
    Up in the air so blue?
Oh, I do think it the pleasantest thing
    Ever a child can do!

Up in the air and over the wall,
    Till I can see so wide,
Rivers and trees and cattle and all
    Over the countryside—

Till I look down on the garden green,
    Down on the roof so brown—
Up in the air I go flying again,
    Up in the air and down!

Robert Louis Stevenson

Frolic & Fancy

A Swing Song

Swing, swing,
Sing, sing,
Here! my throne and I am a King!
Swing, sing,
Swing, sing,
Farewell, earth, for I'm on the wing!

Low, high,
Here I fly,
Like a bird through sunny sky;
Free, free,
Over the lea,
Over the mountain, over the sea!

Up, down,
Up and down,
Which is the way to London Town?
Where? Where?
Up in the air,
Close your eyes, and now you are there!

Soon, soon,
Afternoon,
Over the sunset, over the moon;
Far, far,
Over the bar,
Sweeping on from star to star!

No, no,
Low, low,
Sweeping daisies with my toe.
Slow, slow,
To and fro,
Slow—
        slow—
                slow—
                        slow.

William Allingham

F r o l i c & F a n c y

Comparing Poems

Tell your class that you are going to read two poems in which the children are doing the same thing. Read "The Swing" and "A Swing Song" aloud and try to evoke the movement of a swing as you read. Ask children to close their eyes as you read and try to visualize the action. After the reading, encourage children to comment on how each poet helps them feel the movement of a swing.

Point out that the title of the second poem is "A Swing Song." Ask children why they feel the poem was given this title. Then ask them how the movement and rhythm of a swing compare to a song.

Discuss with children the fact that both poems are about the same subject. Ask them to compare the action of swinging in both poems. Then invite children to share their opinions about which poem "feels" more like swinging and which they enjoyed more and why.

Ready for Action

Make copies of the poems on pages 18 and 19 and distribute them to children, or print them on the chalkboard. Invite one half of the class to read the poems in unison as the other half moves to the sound and rhythm of the words. Readers may wish to move back and forth as if they were on a swing or in any way they choose that represents the sound and rhythm of the words.

Verb Poems

Explain to children that action can be expressed in the words and rhythm of poems like "The Swing" and "A Swing Song." Ask children if they know what action words are called. Explain that in one kind of poem, called a *verb poem,* the letters of the action word or words are arranged to look like the word's meaning. Print the following examples on the chalkboard.

stepping   circling   jumping jumping jumping

Allow children time to think of some action words that could be used to form verb poems. Then distribute drawing paper and invite children to create their own verb poems.

Frolic & Fancy

Picture Poetry

Explain to children that sometimes poems are written so that they actually look like the objects they are describing. These poems are called *concrete poems*. Print the following concrete poem on the chalkboard.

```
slink
     ing,
         slith
              ering,
                   s
                   lid
                      ing,
                          slippery, slee py, snak y, snak e
```

Help children to read the poem, emphasizing the alliteration. Explain that concrete poems can take any shape and that they can be read or just looked at.
   Have children brainstorm the objects or animals they would like to depict in a concrete poem. Provide drawing paper, and let children choose subjects and create their own concrete poems.

An Art Gallery of Poems

When they have finished, display children's concrete poems along the chalkboard ledge and elsewhere around the classroom so that the room looks like an art gallery. Direct the class's attention to one poem at a time, and have the poet stand next to his or her work. If the poem is meant to be read, ask the poet to read it. Then encourage the poet to explain what the poem portrays and why he or she chose the shape to portray it.

Frolic & Fancy

Name _____ Date _____

Monster Description Sheet

Write answers to the following questions.
What does your monster look like?

_____

_____

_____

How does your monster move?

_____

_____

_____

What sounds does your monster make?

_____

_____

What does it do?

_____

_____

Is there anything your monster likes or doesn't like?

_____

_____

What do you call your monster?

_____

On a separate sheet of paper, write a poem using your answers.

Frolic & Fancy

Name _____ Date _____

Riddle _____

1. I look _____, _____, and _____.

2. I feel _____

   _____.

3. I smell _____

   and taste _____.

4. You can find me _____

   _____.

5. You can eat me _____

   _____.

Now write a *riddle poem* about an apple, using what you wrote above.
Your poem should describe the apple without telling what it is. Let your
reader guess!

23

Frolic & Fancy

Name _____ Date _____

Limerick

A *limerick* is a short, humorous five-line poem. Its first, second, and fifth lines rhyme. The third and fourth lines also rhyme. A poet named Edward Lear (1812–88) made limericks very popular many years ago. Here is one of Lear's limericks:

> There is a young lady whose nose
> Continually prospers and grows;
>   When it grew out of sight,
>   She exclaimed in a fright,
> "Oh, Farewell to the end of my nose."

You can write limericks of your own. Use Edward Lear's limerick as a model and use a similar rhythm and rhyme pattern. Use the starter sentence below as the first line of your limerick, or write your own, if you wish. Be as funny or silly as you can be!

There was a young boy from Kerfew,

_____

_____

_____

_____

24

Tasty Treats

Children will begin to think of their favorite delicious foods as they read the poems in this unit. First, they will encounter a modern-day Hansel and Gretel and a witch who fattens them up on a diet of broccoli and apple juice. A comparison of the poem "Life In The Forest. Or: Bad News . . . Good News . . . Bad News. . . ." with the fairy tale "Hansel and Gretel" will provoke thought about healthful foods. Subsequent art and writing activities let children create their own balanced meals. The creative process continues as children follow up their reading of "The Bakers" by writing poems so rhythmic that a ball can be bounced to them. Children will then read fanciful rhymes as well as some tongue-twisting verses that describe the fascinations of food. After meeting the ecstatic narrator of "Beautiful Soup," readers will even be invited to make their own Stone Soup.

The poetry in this unit is excellent "food for thought," and the classroom activities and Activity Sheets that accompany the poems are sure to give children an appetite for fun and learning!

Where to Find More Poems

Adoff, Arnold. **Chocolate Dreams.** Lothrop, Lee & Shepard, 1989.

Ciardi, John. **Doodle Soup.** Houghton Mifflin, 1985.

Merriam, Eve. **A Poem for a Pickle.** Morrow, 1989.

Tasty Treats

Life In The Forest.
Or: Bad News . . .
    Good News . . .
Bad News. . . .

First: Hansel and Gretel try to follow
a trail of chocolate chips and chocolate-
covered raisins back to their home.
But the sun melts the chips, and the tiny
pools of chocolate are licked up by
chocolate chip–loving chipmunks. And the
raisins are pecked up by the birds
who usually eat boring bread crumbs in
              this
             story.

So they become hopelessly lost
and end up at the candy house of the
wicked
witch who captures them both.   But
                the

wicked
witch is so wicked that she feeds them
on a strict diet of broccoli and apple
juice, and they both become so big and
strong that they break out of their cages,
push the mean witch into an oven full of
toasted tofu tarts, and run away back
             home.
Upon hearing the wondrous tale of their
broccoli behavior and escape, their
parents vow to buy only broccoli and
apple juice forevermore. And Hansel
          and
         Gretel
are put to work chopping wood to pay
for all this green goodness. Healthy
and tired and sad, they fall asleep
each night so hungry for a brown morsel
of mouth-melting chocolate . . . thinking of
the candy house in the forest . . . and the
kindly face
      of the
smiling
witch.

Arnold Adoff

Tasty Treats

From Fairy Tale to Poetry

Obtain a brief version of the fairy tale "Hansel and Gretel" and read it aloud to children. Tell them that next you are going to read a poem that is also about Hansel and Gretel, but the tale that is told in the poem is quite different from the traditional fairy tale. Read aloud "Life In The Forest. Or: Bad News . . . Good News . . . Bad News. . . ." Ask children to tell how the title summarizes the events in the poem. Discuss how the story in the poem differs from the traditional fairy tale version. You may wish to use the following questions to guide the discussion:

- Compare and contrast the story "Hansel and Gretel" with the story in "Life In The Forest. Or: Bad News . . . Good News . . . Bad News. . . ." Which story did you prefer? Why?
- Which parts of the poem did you find funny?
- If you could speak to the poet, Arnold Adoff, what would you want to tell him or ask him?
- If you could have a feast now that you've heard the poem, what would you want to eat?

Dramatizing a Poem

Invite children to work in small groups to do dramatic interpretations of the poem. Ask them to choose roles and write dialogue and narration. Allow them time for rehearsal, and when they are ready, let the groups take turns presenting their playlets.

A Unique Pairing of Words

Point out the phrase *broccoli behavior* in the poem and ask children what they think it means. Explain that in poetry, authors often put words together in a way that is not heard in everyday language. In so doing, poets describe things in vivid and unusual ways.

Tasty Treats

Poems with Two-Word Lines

Explain to children that in a poem with two-word lines, each line has only two words. The poem can be any length, but each line tells something different about the poem's subject. Write the following poems on the chalkboard.

New coat   Dirty sneakers
Dark blue   Snaky laces
Shiny buttons   Holey toes
Toasty warm   Smelly soles
Cold outside   Thrown away
Almost winter   Good riddance!
I'm ready

Invite children to write their own poems with two-word lines, illustrate them, and share them with the class.

Nutritious and Delicious

Begin a discussion about the kinds of foods the witch feeds Hansel and Gretel in the poem (broccoli, apple juice). Ask children how the poet feels about these foods and how they can tell. Invite them to share their opinions of the foods mentioned in the poem. Then ask them to name some of their favorite foods. Write the headings *Meat and Eggs*, *Milk and Dairy*, *Cereals and Grains*, and *Fruits and Vegetables* on the board and write students' favorite foods under the appropriate categories.

Distribute a copy of the Balanced Meal Activity Sheet (page 40). Invite children to plan a balanced breakfast, lunch, and dinner, and to write poems about the meals.

Creating a Balanced Meal

For this activity each child will need a legal-sized sheet of construction paper, a white paper plate, a paper cup, and a paper napkin. First, have children take a look at the sample balanced meals they made on the Balanced Meal Activity Sheet. Distribute the art materials and ask children to glue or staple the paper plate, cup, and napkin to the construction-paper place mat. Encourage them to draw the foods they have selected to make a balanced meal on the paper plate. Children may draw a breakfast, lunch, or dinner. When they have finished, invite children to explain their meals and tell why they are balanced.

Tasty Treats

The Bakers

Bridget baked some biscuits,
Some biscuits, some biscuits.
Bridget baked some biscuits
And Betsey baked a bun.
Bella baked some brownies,
Some brownies, some brownies.
Bella baked some brownies
And Bessie's beans are done.
Barbara only bounced her ball,
Bounced her ball, bounced her ball.
Barbara only bounced her ball.
She simply cannot cook at all.

Lee Blair

Meter Moves

After reading "The Bakers," ask children if the way some of the words repeat and the strong rhythm pattern make them feel like moving in a special way. Invite children to demonstrate their own movements as they take turns reading the poem aloud.

Bounce to the Beat

Demonstrate how the poem can be read in time to bouncing a small rubber ball. Invite children to work in small groups. Provide each group with a ball and encourage them to make up their own ball-bouncing games as they chant the words in the poem.

Poems to Bounce By

Invite children to make up original verses to which they can also bounce a ball. Allow them time to experiment with the rhythm and alliterative qualities of "The Bakers" and apply them to original verses. When they are finished, invite them to chant their verses and demonstrate the ball games they devised.

Tasty Treats

Bubble, Bubble, Bubble

"Bubble," said the kettle,
"Bubble," said the pot.
"Bubble, bubble, bubble,
We are getting very hot!"

Shall I take you off the fire?
"No, you need not trouble.
This is just the way we talk—
Bubble, bubble, bubble!"

Anonymous

One Day a Boy Went Walking

One day a boy went walking
And went into a store.
He bought a pound of sausages
And laid them on the floor.

The boy began to whistle
A merry little tune—
And all the little sausages
Danced around the room!

Anonymous

I Eat My Peas with Honey

I eat my peas with honey;
I've done it all my life.
It makes the peas taste funny,
But it keeps them on the knife.

Anonymous

Tasty Treats

Quatrain

Explain to children that one common form of poetry is a *quatrain*. A quatrain has four lines with any kind of rhythm. Usually the last line rhymes with the second or third line, but there can be other kinds of rhyme schemes. Explain that "I Eat My Peas with Honey" is one quatrain alone, and "Bubble, Bubble, Bubble" and "One Day a Boy Went Walking" are both two quatrains put together. Read the poems again and help children identify the quatrains and the rhyme scheme in each ("Bubble, Bubble, Bubble" and "One Day a Boy Went Walking" *abcb*; "I Eat My Peas with Honey" *abab*).

Read the following couplet aloud and invite children to compose the next two lines.

> My sister picked a flower
> Of a pretty shade of pink;

If necessary, suggest that they try for an *abab* or *abcb* rhyme scheme. When children feel comfortable with the form of the quatrain, invite pairs to experiment with other rhyme schemes and write their own quatrains.

Foods Come Alive!

Read "Bubble, Bubble, Bubble" and "One Day a Boy Went Walking" to your class. Ask them to point out the instances in each poem when objects or foods move or talk. Then encourage them to write their own poems about their favorite foods coming alive before their eyes. Have them think about how fond they are of their favorite foods, and ask them, "If you could tell your favorite food anything you'd like, what would you say? How do you think it would reply?"

How Can You EAT That?!

Invite children to read "I Eat My Peas with Honey" aloud with you. Ask them if they enjoy unusual combinations of foods, and encourage them to share times when they have tried unusual foods for the first time.

Tasty Treats

A CUPBOARDFUL OF TASTY POEMS

Peter Piper

Peter Piper picked a peck of pickled peppers;
A peck of pickled peppers Peter Piper picked.
If Peter Piper picked a peck of pickled peppers,
Where's the peck of pickled peppers Peter Piper picked?

Mother Goose

Betty Botter's Butter

Betty Botter bought some butter,
"But," she said, "the butter's bitter.
If I put it in my batter,
It will make my batter bitter.
But a bit of better butter,
That would make my batter better."
So she bought a bit of butter
Better than her bitter butter,
And she put it in her batter
And the batter was not bitter.
So 'twas better Betty Botter
Bought a bit of better butter.

Anonymous

Pease Porridge

Pease porridge hot,
   Pease porridge cold,
Pease porridge in the pot,
   Nine days old.

Some like it hot,
   Some like it cold,
Some like it in the pot,
   Nine days old.

Mother Goose

Through the Teeth

Through the teeth
And past the gums
Look out stomach,
Here it comes!

Folk Rhyme

I Scream, You Scream

I scream, you scream,
We all scream
For ice cream!

Traditional

Tasty Treats

Let's Alliterate

Read "Peter Piper" and "Betty Botter's Butter" to children. Discuss the story line in each poem and help children to understand the humor. Define *alliteration* as the repeating pattern of consonant sounds, especially at the beginning of words. Ask children what sounds are repeated in "Peter Piper," "Betty Botter's Butter," and "Pease Porridge." Tell children that the use of alliteration sometimes helps to make a poem funny, and also seems to make the words in a poem jump out at us.

To make another interesting observation, point out that "Betty Botter's Butter" uses five similar words and that each has a different vowel sound (batter, better, bitter, Botter, butter).

Invite children to work with a partner. Ask the pairs to choose an initial consonant sound and write a short poem about food that contains alliteration.

Twist Your Tongue

Children will enjoy reading "Peter Piper" and "Betty Botter's Butter" aloud. Point out that alliteration often helps to make a poem a tongue twister. Once they are familiar with the words, challenge children to take turns reading these tongue twisters as fast as they can. Then, invite them to read aloud their original alliteration poems.

Advertisements with Puns

Point out that in "I Scream, You Scream," the phrase "I Scream" is a *pun*. Define a pun as a word or phrase that is used cleverly so that it sounds like it has more than one meaning. (In the poem, "I scream" sounds just like "ice cream.") Puns are often used in advertisements because they are humorous and catchy.

Invite children to work in pairs and provide each pair with several magazines. Encourage them to cut out ads that contain puns or other catchy phrases and paste them onto a sheet of drawing paper, leaving some space in the center of the page. Then invite children to write their own advertisements for their favorite foods in the center of the ad collage.

Tasty Treats

The Man in the Onion Bed

I met a man in an onion bed.
He was crying so hard his eyes were red.
And the tears ran off the end of his nose
As he ate his way down the onion rows.

He ate and he cried, but for all his tears
He sang: "Sweet onions, oh my dears!
I love you, I do, and you love me,
But you make me as sad as a man can be."

John Ciardi

Onion Tears and Onion Dears

Hold a discussion about what children think contributes to the humor in "The Man in the Onion Bed." Point out that in the last three lines, the poet gives human attributes to onions, which are inanimate objects. Explain that giving inanimate objects human traits is called *personification*. Encourage children to describe how the man speaks to the onions as if they were people.

Then ask what natural characteristics onions have. Someone is bound to point out that the fumes from onions often bring tears to people's eyes. At that point, you may wish to point out that another feature of the poem that contributes to the humor is the fact that onions really can make people cry, but *not* because they make people sad.

Tasty Treats

Cinquain

Write the following poems on the chalkboard:

Pumpkin
Halloween face
Candle lights inside shell
Glowing eyes are frightening, strange
Lantern

Rainbow
Cheerful ribbon
Arches across the sky
Makes me glad the rain has fallen
Colors

A *cinquain* is a form of poetry that contains five lines. In this poetic form, the first and fifth lines contain two syllables, the second line has four syllables, the third line has six syllables, and the fourth line has eight syllables. Clap out the syllables in your name as you say it aloud. Then have children clap out the syllables in each line of the cinquains and write the number next to each line.

Point out to children that there are some other rules for each line of a cinquain. Write the following list on the chalkboard:

First line: title
Second line: description of the title
Third line: action
Fourth line: feeling
Fifth line: another word for the title

Measure the cinquains against the list of rules. When you feel that children understand the technique for writing a cinquain, encourage them to create one as a class. Have a volunteer write the class's cinquain on the chalkboard.

Writing Cinquains

Distribute the Cinquain Activity Sheet on page 41. Invite children to read the directions and have fun writing their own cinquains. Favorite foods are sure to make good subjects for the poems. When children have finished, encourage several volunteers to share their work with the rest of the class.

Tasty Treats

Beautiful Soup

Beautiful Soup, so rich and green,

Waiting in a hot tureen!

Who for such dainties would not stoop?

Soup of the evening, beautiful Soup!

Soup of the evening, beautiful Soup!

   Beau—ootiful Soo—oop!

   Beau—ootiful Soo—oop!

Soo—oop of the e—e—evening,

   Beautiful, beautiful Soup!

Beautiful Soup! Who cares for fish,

Game, or any other dish?

Who would not give all else for two

pennyworth only of beautiful Soup?

Pennyworth only of beautiful Soup?

   Beau—ootiful Soo—oop!

   Beau—ootiful Soo—oop!

Soo—oop of the e—e—evening,

   Beautiful, beauti—FUL SOUP!

Lewis Carroll

Tasty Treats

Choral Reading

Read "Beautiful Soup" aloud two or three times so children can appreciate the rhythm, rhyme, and repetition of the words and lines. Print the poem on the chalkboard or distribute a copy of the poem to each child. Encourage them to read it silently as you read it again orally. Ask children to describe the images evoked by the rhythm and repetition of the words. Call their attention to the repetition of the long u sound, and point out that it adds both a musical sound and humor to the poem.

   When children are familiar with the poem, have the class read it aloud in unison. Encourage them to recite expressively so that they re-create the sound of someone thoroughly enjoying steaming, hot soup.

Prose to Poetry

Explain to children that poetic writing can be found in some unlikely places. For example, they might read a passage such as the following on the food page of a newspaper. Read the passage aloud to students.

   Many people feel that there is absolutely nothing like soup. Nothing makes one feel so comforted and just plain well cared for. The luscious aroma of cooking soup hugs a whole house and invites family and friends into the kitchen for, perhaps, a little taste.

Encourage children to work in small groups. Have them write poems based on the prose passage and share them with the class.

Newspaper and Magazine Poems

Invite children to work in pairs. Distribute cookbooks or the food pages from newspapers and magazines to each pair. Ask them to skim several articles until they find one that contains interesting or poetic writing. Then tell them to underline words, phrases, or sentences that particularly appeal to the senses. Suggest that children arrange the words and phrases into poems. When the poems are finished, invite the pairs to read their excerpts and poems aloud. You may also wish to display their work on a wall or bulletin board.

Tasty Treats

Let's Make Stone Soup!

There are several versions of the folk tale "Stone Soup." Obtain one and read it aloud to your class. Begin a discussion by asking children how the hungry main characters were able to convince the townspeople to help make soup. Help children to understand the irony in the story. Finally, review the ingredients the characters used to make Stone Soup.

Tell children that they, too, can make soup from a stone. To make enough stone soup for approximately 20 servings, you will need the following ingredients:

Stone Soup

1 large stone that has been
    scrubbed clean
5 cups (1¼ liters) chicken soup
about 20 cups (5 liters) water
10 chicken bouillon cubes
3 large onions, chopped
6 cups (1½ liters) chopped raw vegetables,
    such as beans, celery, zucchini, carrots,
    cabbage, spinach, and potatoes
3 cups (750 ml) raw rice

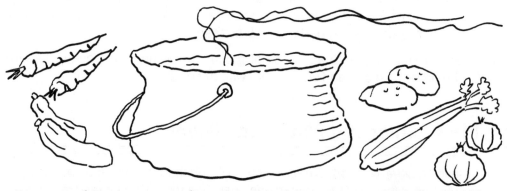

Put everything into a very large pot. Put the soup over a high flame and bring to a boil. Stir gently. Simmer for about 20 minutes or until the vegetables are tender and the rice is cooked. Test by tasting. Add salt and pepper as desired. Serve with bread and butter.

In the folk tale, making the soup was a collective effort. After children have washed their hands, let them each throw in a piece of vegetable. During the meal, have them think about the soup's contents and how good it tastes. After the meal, have children write a poem about Stone Soup.

Tasty Treats

The Limerick Song

If possible, play "The Limerick Song" for your class, singing the limerick verses as you play. Invite children to sing along with you or recite the limericks. Then encourage children to work in groups to create other silly limericks about food and sing them, using the melody from "The Limerick Song."

1. A man who was din-ing at Crewe _____ Found quite a large
2. There was an old man from Pe-ru _____ Who dreamed he was

mouse in his stew; _____ Said the wait-er, "Don't shout ___ And ___
eat-ing his shoe. _____ When he woke in a fright In the ___

wave it a-bout, Or the rest will be want-ing one too!"_____
dark of the night, ___ He found it was per-fect-ly true. _____

Tasty Treats

Name _____ Date _____

Balanced Meal

FOOD GROUPS

Milk and Dairy	*Fruits and Vegetables*	*Meat and Eggs*	*Cereals and Grains*
ice cream, cream, cheese, butter, cream cheese, cottage cheese	peaches, plums, apples, oranges, spinach, broccoli, carrots, beans, potatoes, tomatoes	beef, pork, chicken, liver, eggs, turkey, goose	rice, barley, grits, wheat bread, rye bread, oatmeal

Plan your own balanced meals. On the lines, write a menu for a balanced breakfast, lunch, and dinner.

BREAKFAST

_____

_____

_____

DINNER

_____

_____

_____

_____

LUNCH

_____

_____

_____

On a separate sheet of paper, write an original poem about a balanced meal you have planned above. Let your poem tell how each food makes the meal balanced and how you feel about eating it.

Tasty Treats

Name _____ Date _____

Cinquain

A cinquain is a five-line poem. Each line must have a certain number of syllables. Each line must also tell something about the title.

SYLLABLES	DESCRIPTION	EXAMPLE
2	title	Rainbow
4	description of title	Cheerful ribbon
6	action	Arches across the sky
8	feeling	Makes me glad the rain has fallen
2	another word for title	Colors

Write two cinquains on the lines below.

_____

_____

_____

_____

_____

_____

_____

_____

_____

Tasty Treats

Name _____ Date _____

The Pancake

Mix a pancake,
Stir a pancake,
  Pop it in the pan;
Fry the pancake,
Toss the pancake—
  Catch it if you can!

Christina Rossetti

Work with a partner. Read "The Pancake" several times until you know it well. Then, on the lines below, write a poem about your favorite food, using the same rhythm and rhyme. Share your work.

_____
(poem's title)

_____

_____

_____

_____

_____

_____

_____

_____

_____

Family & Friends

The snug, safe haven of home, filled with family and friends, is at the heart of the poetry in this unit. Children will meet a peer who has a bothersome little brother. They will read about what is special to a young child about home. Perhaps children will think about their own parents when they read about two special people who have divergent interests but something important in common—their love for each other and for their child.

Young readers will meet some interesting family "characters," such as Aunt Selina, who comes for a visit and makes the narrator wonder what she must have been like as a child. Then they will travel to Grandfather's house for a Thanksgiving celebration, singing a favorite song as they go. This is sure to remind children of special times throughout the year when they get together with family and friends to share important occasions.

While family is the focus of the first part of "Family & Friends," friendship is the focus of the latter part. Readers will meet five boys who are the very best of friends, content to be together even when doing nothing. Youngsters will also have the opportunity to contemplate other children who live in faraway places but, like themselves, share the love of close families and good friends.

Where to Find More Poems

Livingston, Myra Cohn. **Poems for Fathers.** Holiday House, 1989.

———. **Poems for Mothers.** Holiday House, 1988.

Prelutsky, Jack. **My Parents Think I'm Sleeping.** Greenwillow, 1985.

Streich, Corrine, ed. **Grandparents' Houses.** Greenwillow, 1984.

Family & Friends

Brother

I had a little brother
And I brought him to my mother
And I said I want another
Little brother for a change.
But she said don't be a bother
So I took him to my father
And I said this little bother
Of a brother's very strange.

But he said one little brother
Is exactly like another
And every little brother
Misbehaves a bit he said.
So I took the little bother
From my mother and my father
And I put the little bother
Of a brother back to bed.

Mary Ann Hoberman

Family & Friends

Relating Poetry to Personal Experience

Read "Brother" aloud to your class. Ask children if there have been times when their siblings were a "bother." Invite them to share personal experiences.

Open a discussion about the rhythm and tongue-twister quality of the language, and challenge children to identify the rhyme scheme *(aaab)*. Encourage several volunteers to read the poem orally. Then ask four children to read four lines each. Repeat with other groups of four.

Paper Bag Puppets

Ask children to think of one specific incident that occurred between themselves and a sibling or siblings—one that evoked a strong emotion. Explain that the incident might have evoked anger, sympathy, laughter, surprise, joy, or sadness. Ask them to think of the family members involved in the incident, including themselves. Provide paper bags, crayons, markers, glue, and scraps of fabric, yarn, and paper, and invite children to make a paper bag puppet that represents each family member who took part in the incident.

Encourage children to work in small groups. Have them show one another their puppets and share the incident that occurred in their families. Then each child can take a turn being the director and organizing other group members to put on a puppet show that depicts their incident. Invite each group to present their puppet shows to the class.

Bother of a Brother?

Ask children to think about what it is like to have a sibling. Give each of them a copy of the Brothers and Sisters Activity Sheet on page 58 and ask them to draw a small picture of an actual or imaginary sibling in the picture frame. Encourage children to list as many words and phrases as they can that describe the sibling, write the words around the picture, and use the words and phrases to write a poem.

Family & Friends

Home! You're Where It's Warm Inside

Home! You are a special place;

you're where I wake and wash my face,

brush my teeth and comb my hair,

change my socks and underwear,

clean my ears and blow my nose,

try on all my parents' clothes.

Home! You're where it's warm inside,

where my tears are gently dried,

where I'm comforted and fed,

where I'm forced to go to bed,

where there's always love to spare;

Home! I'm glad that you are there.

Jack Prelutsky

Family & Friends

Home Sweet Home

Read "Home! You're Where It's Warm Inside" and ask children to compare how the narrator feels about home with their own special feelings about home. Encourage several volunteers to read the poem aloud and ask children to identify the rhyme scheme *(aabbcc)*. Explain that when two lines in a poem have a complementary rhythm and the last words rhyme, the lines form a *couplet*. Read these couplets aloud and ask children to identify the rhyming words.

> Wherever I roam,
> There's no place like home.
>
> Rain, rain, go away,
> Come again some other day.

Couplet Coup

Suggest some pairs of rhyming words such as *part/heart, crumble/grumble, find/mind, giggle/wiggle,* and invite children to create their own couplets.

Home Poems

Distribute copies of the Rhyme Time Activity Sheet on page 59. After children have written as many rhyming words as they can, invite them to use some of the rhyming words, or others, in a poem consisting of couplets. Encourage them to write about their home and what they like to do there.

Dream Rooms

Give each child an empty shoe box, clay, construction paper, and a variety of art materials such as fabric and yarn scraps, foil, cardboard, and so on. Invite children to use the materials to create dioramas that show what their "dream room" would look like if they had a whole room in their homes to decorate. Encourage them to be fanciful. Invite children to display their rooms and tell about some of the special features they included.

Family & Friends

Two People

She reads the paper,
while he turns on TV;
she likes the mountains,
he craves the sea.

He'd rather drive,
she'll take the plane;
he waits for sunshine;
she walks in the rain.

He gulps down cold drinks,
she sips at hot;
he asks, "Why go?"
She asks, "Why not?"

In just about everything
they disagree,
but they love one another
and they both love me.

Eve Merriam

Zuñi Grandfather

My grandfather
how have you been passing the days?
Happily, as old as I am
I could be grandfather to anyone
for we
have many children

Zuñi grandfather poem

Zuñi Grandmother

Grandmother of mine
how have you been passing the days?
Happily, our child
surely I could be grandmother
to anyone
for we
have the whole village as our children

Zuñi grandmother poem

Family & Friends

Aunt Selina

When Aunt Selina comes to tea

She always makes them send for me,

And I must be polite and clean

And seldom heard, but always seen.

I must sit stiffly in my chair

As long as Aunt Selina's there.

But there are certain things I would

Ask Aunt Selina if I could.

I'd ask when she was small, like me,

If she had ever climbed a tree.

Of if she'd ever, ever gone

Without her shoes and stockings on

Where lovely puddles lay in rows

To let the mud squeeze through her toes.

Of if she'd coasted on a sled,

Or learned to stand upon her head

And wave her feet—and after that

I'd ask her how she got so fat.

These things I'd like to ask, and then—

I hope she would not come again!

Carol Haynes

Family & Friends

Which Two People?

After reading aloud "Two People," ask children if they know two people like those in the poem, and invite them to tell who they are. Encourage them to imagine what various daily activities, such as dinner time or free time in the evening, are like for the family in the poem.

Characters in Poetry

Point out that poems, like stories, can describe characters. Ask children to compare and contrast the characters described in "Two People," the Zuñi grandparent poems, and "Aunt Selina."

Interviewing a Family Member

Give each child a copy of the Family Interview Activity Sheet on page 60 and encourage them to think about a family member they would like to know more about. Ask them to use the questions on the Activity Sheet as the basis for an interview. Suggest that they create some of their own questions as well.

Story Poem

With the information from the Family Interview, children can create a poem that tells a story about the family member. Suggest that children begin by substituting more colorful or poetic words for some of the words in the answers on the Activity Sheet.

Family Anecdote and Family Album

Ask children to think of a funny, happy, silly, or important event that took place in their families. Then ask them to write a poem that describes the incident. Give each child two sheets of drawing paper and, if necessary, demonstrate how to fold the paper to make a four-page booklet. Children can draw one picture on each page to illustrate the family anecdote. Encourage them to make the first page a cover like one they might see on a family photo album.

Family & Friends

Address Poems

Each child starts by writing his or her address in a vertical column. Explain to children that next to each number, they should write a line that contains that number of words and/or syllables. Next to each letter, they should write a word that begins with the letter. Use the following address poem as an example.

12 S.E. Park St.

1 child
2 grown-ups
S sit
E eating
P pastry
A and
R reading
K kids'
S silly
T tales

Family Mobiles

Give each child a wire hanger, several lengths of yarn, and drawing paper and crayons. Invite children to make drawings of several family members. Then have them cut out the drawings, attach pieces of yarn to them, and tie the other end of each piece of yarn to the hanger.

Togetherness Poems

Invite children to write poems that tell about something their families do together or something they enjoy doing with family members. Children can illustrate their work and share it with the class. You may wish to display the poems on a wall or bulletin board.

Family & Friends

Thanksgiving Day

Over the river and through the wood,
  To grandfather's house we go:
    The horse knows the way
    To carry the sleigh
  Through the white and drifted snow.

Over the river and through the wood—
  Oh, how the wind does blow!
    It stings the toes
    And bites the nose,
  As over the ground we go.

Over the river and through the wood,
  To have a first-rate play.
    Hear the bells ring,
    "Ting-a-ling-ding!"
  Hurrah for Thanksgiving Day!

Over the river and through the wood
  Trot fast, my dapple-gray!
    Spring, over the ground,
    Like a hunting-hound!
  For this is Thanksgiving Day.

Over the river and through the wood,
  And straight through the barn-yard gate.
    We seem to go
    Extremely slow—
  It is so hard to wait!

Over the river and through the wood—
  My grandmother's cap I spy!
    Hurrah for the fun!
    Is the pudding done?
  Hurrah for the pumpkin-pie!

Lydia Maria Child

Read It, Sing It

Tell your class that you are going to read a poem that describes how a child of long ago felt about Thanksgiving. Invite children to share their feelings about this holiday. As you read "Thanksgiving Day" aloud, ask them to listen for details about the journey and the upcoming celebration as they enjoy the lyric quality of the poem.

You may want to explain to children that this poem is often sung. If you or any members of the class know the melody, sing the song together. Then invite the rest of the class to join in as you sing "Thanksgiving Day" again.

Happy Thanksgiving!

Give children a chance to explain how they celebrate Thanksgiving and what aspects of the celebration are traditional. Then ask children how they think the narrator of "Thanksgiving Day" feels about the holiday. Encourage them to compare and contrast the anticipated celebration in the poem with contemporary Thanksgiving celebrations.

Happiness Is . . .

Distribute old magazines, scissors, paste, and large sheets of paper to each child. Encourage children to look through the magazines to find pictures of things that make them happy or thankful. They can cut out the pictures and paste them on the background paper to make a collage. When the collages are finished, ask children to jot down some words and phrases that describe some of the pictured objects and how they inspire happiness. Invite children to use the words and phrases to write a poem about happiness or thankfulness. They can take turns displaying their collages and reading their poems.

Family & Friends

My Four Friends

I live in an apartment house
next to a vacant lot,
my buddies live there also,
the four best friends I've got.

There's Tony and there's Lumpy
and there's Harvey and there's Will,
and we all hang out together
in the middle of our hill.

Tony's always cheerful,
I think he's really neat
although he wears thick glasses
and is clumsy on his feet.

Lumpy causes trouble,
he's the terror of the block,
he gets away with plenty
'cause he's just too small to sock.

Harvey's mean and nasty,
he's selfish as a pig,
but no one ever hits him
'cause Harvey's just too big.

Will is sort of special,
he acts like a chimpanzee,
I like Will an awful lot
'cause Will's a lot like me.

Sometimes
    we have races,
and sometimes
    we play ball,
but mostly
    we're just buddies
doing nothing
    much at all.

Jack Prelutsky

Other Children

Some children live in palaces
Behind an iron gate
And go to sleep in beds of gold
Whenever it gets late.

Some other children live in tents
With feathers all around
And take their naps in blankets
That are spread upon the ground.

And way up north the children live
In houses built of ice
And think that beds made out of fur
Are really very nice.

In countries where the nights are hot,
Without a single breeze,
The children sleep on bamboo beds
That fasten to the trees.

Some day I think I'll travel 'round
And visit every land
And learn to speak the language that
Each child can understand.

They'll teach me how to play their games
And, if they want me to,
I'll show them diff'rent kinds of tricks
That I know how to do.

They'll want to ask me questions then
And I will ask them others,
Until at last we understand
Like sisters and like brothers.

Helen Wing

Family & Friends

Friends 'Til the End

Read aloud "My Four Friends" and "Other Children," two poems about friendship. Ask children to close their eyes and visualize what is happening in each poem as you read them aloud again. Discuss the narrator's attitude toward friendship in "My Four Friends." Then have children compare that viewpoint with the viewpoint of the narrator of "Other Children." Ask them which outlook most closely expresses how they feel about being a friend and making new friends.

Choral Reading

Make copies of "My Four Friends" and "Other Children" for each child and ask the class to read silently as you read the poems aloud. Have children do a choral reading of the poems either by dividing the class in half and asking each group to take turns reading stanzas aloud, or asking children for suggestions about forming groups for choral reading.

Pen Pal Poems

Pose the following question: How can the narrator in "Other Children" become friends with children who live in faraway places? Mention that one way for people who live far away from each other to become friendly is by writing letters. Explain that pen pals are friends who correspond through the mail. Invite children to share experiences they have had writing and receiving pen pal letters.

Point out that one alternative to writing letters might be to send and receive pen pal poems. Invite children to work in pairs and think about what they would like to tell a pen pal. Suggest that they jot down their ideas. Then have them use their notes to create a poem. Point out that the poems can be any length and may or may not rhyme, but should give an idea of some of the things that are happening in their lives and tell about things they are doing.

Children can illustrate their poems. Encourage volunteers to share their work with the class. You may wish to arrange an exchange of pen pal poems with another class or another school. You can also display children's work on a wall or bulletin board entitled "Let's communicate!"

Family & Friends

The More We Get Together

Sing "The More We Get Together" for your class. Invite children to sing along once they are familiar with the melody and words. Then encourage children to work in groups to create additional verses that could be sung to the same melody.

The more we get to-geth-er, to-geth-er, to-geth-er,

The more we get to-geth-er, the hap-pier we'll be.

'Cause your friends are my friends, and my friends are your friends. The

more we get to-geth-er, the hap-pier we'll be.

Family & Friends

Name _____ Date _____

Brothers and Sisters

Draw a picture of a sister or brother in the frame. Then write words that tell about him or her on the lines.

_____   _____   _____

_____   _____

_____   _____

_____   _____

_____   _____   _____

On the back, write a poem about the brother or sister you described. Draw a picture to go with your poem.

58

Family & Friends

Name _____ Date _____

Rhyme Time

In each box, write a word. On the lines, write some words that rhyme with each of the words you wrote.

☐	☐	☐

_____   _____   _____
_____   _____   _____
_____   _____   _____
_____   _____   _____

☐	☐	☐

_____   _____   _____
_____   _____   _____
_____   _____   _____
_____   _____   _____

On the back of this sheet, use some of the rhyming words you wrote to write a poem about home.

Family & Friends

Name _____ Date _____

Family Interview

Ask a family member to answer each question. Then use the answers to write a poem.

1. Where were you born? _____
   _____

2. Where did you grow up? _____
   _____

3. Name one special event you remember from your childhood. _____
   _____
   _____

4. How do you spend a typical day? _____
   _____
   _____

5. What do you like to do in your free time? _____
   _____
   _____

6. Name two things that are very special to you and tell why. _____
   _____
   _____
   _____

Featuring Creatures

The incredible and vast realm of the animal kingdom inspires the selections in this unit. Children will meet some of Edward Lear's alphabet animal friends and then read an anonymous poem that uses every letter of the alphabet to begin animal names. They will have fun imagining what Lewis Carroll's Jabberwock might look like and, after being tickled by Carroll's nonsense, will create their own portmanteau words. A poem about a cricket and an ant will inspire a comparison with a similar story in Aesop's fable "The Grasshopper and the Ant."

Children will read a variety of poems that observe animal behavior. Some of these are serious and reverent; others are humorous, chantable rhymes. Readers will become reacquainted with the well-known poor old woman who swallowed a fly and create their own epitaphs for her tombstone. Finally, Christina Rossetti's poem "Hurt No Living Thing" might inspire them to think about what we can do to save animals from extinction so that interesting and wonderful creatures will remain to inhabit the world of the future.

Where to Find More Poems

Carle, Eric. **Animals, Animals.** Philomel, 1989.

Goldstein, Bobbye S., ed. **Bear in Mind: A Book of Bear Poems.** Viking, 1989.

Hooper, Patricia. **A Bundle of Beasts.** Houghton Mifflin, 1987.

Larrick, Nancy, ed. **Cats Are Cats.** Philomel, 1988.

Lewis, J. Patrick. **A Hippopotamusn't and Other Animal Verses.** Dial, 1990.

Featuring Creatures

Animal ABCs

B was once a little bear,
    Beary,
    Wary,
    Hairy,
    Beary,
    Taky cary,
    Little bear!

E was once a little eel,
    Eely,
    Weely,
    Peely,
    Eely,
    Twirly, tweely,
    Little eel!

H was once a little hen,
    Henny,
    Chenny,
    Tenny,
    Henny,
    Eggsy-any,
    Little hen?

M was once a little mouse,
    Mousy,
    Bousy,
    Sousy,
    Mousy,
    In the housy,
    Little mouse!

W was once a whale,
    Whaly,
    Scaly,
    Shaly,
    Whaly,
    Tumbly-taily,
    Mighty whale!

Edward Lear
from "A Was Once an Apple Pie"

An Animal Alphabet

Alligator, beetle, porcupine, whale,
Bobolink, panther, dragonfly, snail,
Crocodile, monkey, buffalo, hare,
Dromedary, leopard, mud-turtle, bear,
Elephant, badger, pelican, ox,
Flying-fish, reindeer, anaconda, fox,
Guinea-pig, dolphin, antelope, goose,
Hummingbird, weasel, pickerel, moose,
Ibex, rhinoceros, owl, kangaroo,
Jackal, opossum, toad, cockatoo,
Kingfisher, peacock, anteater, bat,
Lizard, ichneumon, honey-bee, rat,
Mockingbird, camel, grasshopper, mouse,
Nightingale, spider, cuttle-fish, grouse,
Ocelot, pheasant, wolverine, auk,
Periwinkle, ermine, katydid, hawk,
Quail, hippopotamus, armadillo, moth,
Rattlesnake, lion, woodpecker, sloth,
Salamander, goldfinch, angleworm, dog,
Tiger, flamingo, scorpion, frog,
Unicorn, ostrich, nautilus, mole,
Viper, gorilla, basilisk, sole,
Whippoorwill, beaver, centipede, fawn,
Xantho, canary, polliwog, swan,
Yellowhammer, eagle, hyena, lark,
Zebra, chameleon, butterfly, shark.

Anonymous

Featuring Creatures

ABC Animal Poems

Tell your class that you are going to read some verses that might make them think about some animals in new ways. Read aloud "Animal ABCs." Ask groups of three or four children to take turns reading the verses aloud.

Try writing a verse or two with the class. Agree on a letter and ask children to suggest animals whose names begin with that letter. Encourage suggestions about real or nonsense words that could evoke the nature of the animal. Have children work in pairs to write ABC animal poems of their own. Provide art materials, and have them illustrate and share their work.

Animal Alphabet

Read "An Animal Alphabet" to children and ask them to pay special attention to the letter that begins each line. Point out that the first letters of the lines form the alphabet. Children may enjoy reading the poem aloud in unison.

Distribute large sheets of drawing paper. Invite children to write the alphabet vertically on the left side of the page. Then challenge them to write the name of an animal next to each letter. Finally, have them turn their animal alphabet into a poem by writing two or three descriptive words next to each animal's name. For example:

Anteater, long, snuffly nose
Bear, lumbering and large
Camel, one hump or two?

Alphabet Animals

Provide children with drawing paper and crayons. Invite them to draw any letter they wish in the center of the page. Then ask them to turn the letter into an animal by adding details such as eyes, nose, mouth, ears, wings, tail, and so on. They may also enjoy writing an animal alphabet verse about the animal they have drawn.

63

Jabberwocky

'Twas brillig, and the slithy toves
   Did gyre and gimble in the wabe:
All mimsy were the borogoves,
   And the mome raths outgrabe.

"Beware the Jabberwock, my son!
   The jaws that bite, the claws that catch!
Beware the Jubjub bird, and shun
   The frumious Bandersnatch!"

He took his vorpal sword in hand:
   Long time the manxome foe he sought—
So rested he by the Tumtum tree,
   And stood awhile in thought.

And, as in uffish thought he stood,
   The Jabberwock, with eyes of flame,
Came whiffling through the tulgey wood,
   And burbled as it came!

One, two! One, two! And through and through
   The vorpal blade went snicker-snack!
He left it dead, and with its head
   He went galumphing back.

"And hast thou slain the Jabberwock?
   Come to my arms, my beamish boy!
O frabjous day! Callooh! Callay!"
   He chortled in his joy.

'Twas brillig, and the slithy toves
   Did gyre and gimble in the wabe:
All mimsy were the borogoves,
   And the mome raths outgrabe.

Lewis Carroll

Featuring Creatures

What Nonsense!

Read aloud "Jabberwocky." Then invite your class to read the poem aloud in unison. Ask children to explain what they think a Jabberwock is, based on the images the language conjures.

Portmanteau Words

Draw a simple picture of a suitcase on the chalkboard and print the word *frumious* beneath it. Ask children what English words seem to be combined to form this nonsense word. (Possibilities include *fuming, furious, fretful*.) Print these words or children's suggestions inside the suitcase.

fuming
furious
fretful

frumious

Explain that the nonsense words in "Jabberwocky" are actually combinations of parts of two or three real words put together. Explain that these combinations are sometimes called *portmanteau words* because a portmanteau is a suitcase and the words are packed together in almost the same way as a tightly packed suitcase might be.

Draw another suitcase on the chalkboard and write the word *toves* beneath it. Invite children to locate *toves* in the poem. Then ask them what two words might have been combined to form this nonsense word. *(toads, doves)* Print children's suggestions in the suitcase. Continue with *slithy, mimsy,* and *whiffling.* (Possible combinations include *slimy/slithering, flimsy/miserable, whistling/sniffling.*)

Pack Your Own Suitcase

Invite students to try writing their own portmanteau words. Distribute a copy of the Portmanteau Words Activity Sheet on page 77 to each student. Explain to children that they will be creating portmanteau words to use in their own nonsense poems about creatures. Invite them to illustrate their poems and take turns reading them aloud. As each child reads his or her poem, encourage the class to describe the creature based on the context and portmanteau words.

Featuring Creatures

The Ant and the Cricket

A silly young cricket, accustomed to sing
Through the warm, sunny months of gay summer and spring,
Began to complain when he found that, at home,
His cupboard was empty, and winter was come.
   Not a crumb to be found
   On the snow-covered ground;
   Not a flower could he see,
   Not a leaf on a tree.
"Oh! what will become," says the cricket, "of me?"

At last, by starvation and famine made bold,
All dripping with wet, and all trembling with cold,
Away he set off to a miserly ant,
To see if, to keep him alive, he would grant
   Him shelter from rain,
   And a mouthful of grain.
   He wished only to borrow;
   He'd repay it tomorrow;
If not, he must die of starvation and sorrow.

Says the ant to the cricket, "I'm your servant and friend,
But we ants never borrow; we ants never lend.
Tell me, dear cricket, did you lay nothing by
When the weather was warm?" Quoth the cricket, "Not I!
   My heart was so light
   That I sang day and night,
   For all nature looked gay."
   "You sang, sir, you say?
Go, then," says the ant, "and dance winter away!"

Thus ending, he hastily lifted the wicket,
And out of the door turned the poor little cricket.
Folks call this a fable. Perhaps it is true.
If you were the ant, then what would you do?

Anonymous; Adapted from Aesop

Featuring Creatures

From Prose to Poetry

Obtain the Aesop fable "The Grasshopper and the Ant," and read it aloud. Explain that the story is called a fable because it teaches a lesson, and point out that the characters in most fables are animals that possess human characteristics. Next, read the poem "The Ant and the Cricket." Have children compare the story line in both versions. Invite children to answer the question in the last line of the poem. Then ask them to comment about the actions of the grasshopper or cricket, and those of the ant(s).

A Skit Based on the Poem

Invite students to work in small groups. Each group can read "The Ant and the Cricket" together and decide how to present it as a skit. Point out that they may alter the story line in order to answer the question in the last line of the poem. Invite them to write dialogue and narration, and to assign parts. Children might also enjoy creating props or very simple costumes that distinguish the characters. Ask the groups to present their versions of "The Ant and the Cricket" to the class.

Creating a Fable

Read several fables including Aesop's fables to the class. Discuss the characters in each as well as the lessons they learned. Then children can work in pairs to write fables of their own. Suggest that the characters be animals and at least one character be taught a lesson. Invite children to illustrate their fables and take turns reading them to the class.

   As an additional challenge, children might enjoy turning their fables into poems. Explain that the poems need not rhyme, but there should be a rhythmic quality to the lines as well as a lyrical feel to the words. When children share their work with the class, encourage the audience to compare the prose fables with the fables in poetry.

Featuring Creatures

Comparisons

As wet as a fish—as dry as a bone;
As live as a bird—as dead as a stone;
As plump as a partridge—as poor as a rat;
As strong as a horse—as weak as a cat;
As hard as a flint—as soft as a mole;
As white as a lily—as black as a coal;
As plain as a staff—as rough as a bear;
As light as a drum—as free as the air;
As heavy as lead—as light as a feather;
As steady as time—uncertain as weather;
As hot as an oven—as cold as a frog;
As gay as a lark—as sick as a dog;
As savage as tigers—as mild as a dove;
As stiff as a poker—as limp as a glove;
As blind as a bat—as deaf as a post;
As cool as a cucumber—as warm as toast;
As flat as a flounder—as round as a ball;
As blunt as a hammer—as sharp as an awl;
As brittle as glass—as tough as gristle;
As neat as a pin—as clean as a whistle;
As red as a rose—as square as a box;
As bold as a thief—as sly as a fox.

Anonymous

The Animal Is . . .

Elephant is a large gray mountain;
Peacock's fan is a pouring fountain.
Polar bear is a heap of ice;
Tiny ants are grains of rice.
Butterfly is a colorful kite;
Crow is a smudge of darkest night.

Anonymous

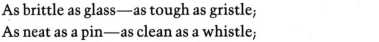

Featuring Creatures

Critter Comparisons

Ask children if they have ever heard expressions such as *happy as a lark, sly as a fox, strong as an ox,* or *wise as an owl.* Invite them to guess what is meant by the phrase *she runs like a jackrabbit.* Then ask whether or not they prefer it to simply saying *she runs quickly.*

Point out that there are many expressions that compare feelings or qualities to animals. Invite children to name other animal comparisons. Explain that when a comparison contains the words *like* or *as,* it is called a *simile.*

Next, invite children to listen for additional animal comparisons as you read "Comparisons." Have volunteers take turns reading a line of the poem aloud. Then talk with children about the feelings or qualities that are being compared, and the objects or animals to which they are being compared.

Metaphor Magic

Explain that another kind of comparison is often made in which something is said to be something else. This comparison is called a *metaphor.* Discuss these metaphors with the class:

> The clouds are fluffy pillows.
> My shoelaces are floppy puppy's ears.
> The still pond is a silver mirror.

Ask children to what the clouds, shoelaces, and pond are being compared. Write "The Animal Is . . ." on the chalkboard. Invite children to read the poem silently first and then aloud in unison, then ask them to react to the metaphors. Have them think of other objects to which the animals could be directly compared.

Write the following on the chalkboard and invite children to fill in the blanks to create their own metaphors:

_____ is _____

_____ is _____

State a Simile, Make a Metaphor

Distribute copies of the Surprising Similes, Magical Metaphors Activity Sheet on page 78. Children can use the illustrations on the page to create similes and metaphors or make up their own. Encourage them to use some of the similes and metaphors they created to write a poem about animals.

Featuring Creatures

Desert Tortoise

I am the *old* one here.

Mice
and snakes
and deer
and butterflies
and badgers
come and go.
Centipedes
and eagles
come and go.

But tortoises
grow old
and *stay.*

Our lives stretch out.

I cross
the same arroyo
that I crossed
when I was young,
returning to
the same safe den
to sleep through
winter's cold.
Each spring,
I warm myself
in the same sun,
search for the same
long tender blades
of green,
and taste the same
ripe juicy cactus fruit.

I know
the slow
sure way
my world
repeats itself.
I know
how I fit in.

My shell still shows
the toothmarks
where a wildcat
thought he had me
long ago.
He didn't know
that I was safe
beneath
the hard brown rock
he tried to bite.

I trust that shell.
I move
at my own speed.

This
is a good place
for an old tortoise
to walk.

Byrd Baylor

Reading "Desert Tortoise"

Before reading "Desert Tortoise," you may wish to explain that an *arroyo* is a gully carved by water found in a dry region such as a desert.

After reading the poem, invite children to share their feelings about the images the poem evokes. Encourage children to describe the tortoise's environment and then ask them to tell how they think the desert tortoise feels about its world and its place in that world.

Creature Sense

If possible, take children on a nature walk, asking them to bring along pencil and paper. Ask children to try to sense their environment by listening to the sounds that emanate from the plant and animal life all around them. Provide a stop during the walk for them to sit quietly and make some notes. Ask them to listen carefully to see if they can hear, see, or sense any of the creatures with whom they share their environment. Invite them to try to put themselves in the place of one of the wild creatures around them and think about how this animal might feel about its surroundings.

After their stop, encourage children to look for stones that are about the size of their palms. These stones will be used to make Rock Turtles (see below).

Creature Voices

Invite children to use their notes to write a poem about how a wild creature living in their locale might experience the world. You may wish to ask them to write from the animal's point of view, and use the lyrical and contemplative tone in "Desert Tortoise" as a model.

Rock Turtles

Display several pictures of turtles and tortoises and encourage children to comment on the different varieties and their appearances. Provide tempera paint, glue, scraps of construction paper and fabric, yarn, and other art materials that are on hand and invite children to create a turtle using the stones they found on the nature walk.

Featuring Creatures

A MENAGERIE OF ANIMAL POEMS

Old Noah's Ark

Old Noah once he built an ark,
And patched it up with hickory bark.
He anchored it to a great big rock,
And then he began to load his stock.
The animals went in one by one,
The elephant chewing a caraway bun.
The animals went in two by two,
The crocodile and the kangaroo.
The animals went in three by three,
The tall giraffe and the tiny flea,
The animals went in four by four,
The hippopotamus stuck in the door.
The animals went in five by five,
The bees mistook the bear for a hive.
The animals went in six by six,
The monkey was up to his usual tricks.
The animals went in seven by seven,
Said the ant to the elephant, "Who're you shov'n?"
The animals went in eight by eight,
Some were early and some were late.
The animals went in nine by nine,
They all formed fours and marched in a line.
The animals went in ten by ten,
If you want any more, you can read it again.

Anonymous

The Eagle

He clasps the crag with crooked hands;
Close to the sun in lonely lands,
Ringed with the azure world, he stands.

The wrinkled sea beneath him crawls;
He watches from his mountain walls,
And like a thunderbolt he falls.

Alfred, Lord Tennyson

The Squirrel

Whisky Frisky,
Hippity hop,
Up he goes
To the tree top!

Whirly, twirly,
Round and round,
Down he scampers
To the ground.

Anonymous

A Centipede

A centipede was happy quite,
  Until a frog in fun
Said, "Pray, which leg comes after which?"
This raised her mind to such a pitch,
She lay distracted in the ditch
  Considering how to run.

Anonymous

I've Got a Dog

I've got a dog as thin as a rail,
He's got fleas all over his tail;
Every time his tail goes flop,
The fleas on the bottom all hop to the top.

Anonymous

The Kangaroo

Old Jumpety-Bumpety-Hop-and-Go-One
Was lying asleep on his side in the sun.
This old kangaroo, he was whisking the flies
(With his long glossy tail) from his ears and his eyes.
Was lying asleep on his side in the sun,
Jumpety-Bumpety-Hop.

Anonymous

Featuring Creatures

Appreciating Animals

Point out to children that poetry about animals can help us to think about animals in new ways. Read aloud some or all of the poems about animals on page 72.

Let the children have fun with the words and the messages. Invite them to comment on aspects of the poetry, such as which poem they thought was the funniest, which caused them to think about an animal in a new way, which poem they liked best and why, and so on.

Old Noah

Encourage children to read aloud "Old Noah's Ark" by selecting a narrator to read the first four lines, the entire class to read the number lines, individuals to read the animal lines, and the whole class to read the last line.

Provide groups with popsicle sticks, crayons, drawing and construction paper, and scraps of fabric, yarn, or decorated paper. Groups can make stick puppets illustrating "Old Noah's Ark." Encourage children to refer to the poem to see how many and what kinds of animal puppets to make. Remind them to include a puppet of Noah and one of the ark. Invite the groups to select someone to read the poem aloud as the rest of the group members stage the puppet show.

Triplets

Print "The Eagle" by Alfred, Lord Tennyson on the chalkboard and invite your class to read it in unison. Point out that there are two three-line stanzas in this poem, and explain that a *triplet* is a stanza of three lines that may or may not rhyme. "The Eagle" is a poem that consists of two triplets.

Triplet Poem

Invite the class to create a triplet poem. Ask children to suggest an animal and write its name on the chalkboard as the poem's title. Then ask children to write three-line stanzas that describe the animal's behavior and appearance. Children can add their stanzas to the chalkboard under the title or put them on paper and post their long triplet poem on the bulletin board.

Featuring Creatures

There Was an Old Woman

There was an old woman, she swallowed a fly.
I don't know why she swallowed a fly.
Perhaps she'll die.

There was an old woman, she swallowed a spider.
It squiggled and wriggled and jiggled inside her.
She swallowed the spider to catch the fly.
I don't know why she swallowed a fly.
Perhaps she'll die.

There was an old woman, she swallowed a bird.
How absurd! She swallowed a bird.
She swallowed the bird to catch the spider,
She swallowed the spider to catch the fly.
I don't know why she swallowed a fly.
Perhaps she'll die.

There was an old woman, she swallowed a cat.
Imagine that! She swallowed a cat.
She swallowed the cat to catch the bird,
She swallowed the bird to catch the spider,
She swallowed the spider to catch the fly.
I don't know why she swallowed a fly.
Perhaps she'll die.

There was an old woman, she swallowed a dog.
She went whole hog when she swallowed the dog.
She swallowed the dog to catch the cat,
She swallowed the cat to catch the bird,
She swallowed the bird to catch the spider,
She swallowed the spider to catch the fly.
I don't know why she swallowed a fly.
Perhaps she'll die.

There was an old woman, she swallowed a cow.
I don't know how she swallowed the cow.
She swallowed the cow to catch the dog,
She swallowed the dog to catch the cat,
She swallowed the cat to catch the bird,
She swallowed the bird to catch the spider,
She swallowed the spider to catch the fly.
I don't know why she swallowed a fly.
Perhaps she'll die.

There was an old woman, she swallowed a horse.
She died, of course!

Anonymous

Featuring Creatures

Sing a Song of Animals

Read "There Was an Old Woman" aloud and invite children to read along with you. Several recordings of this song have been made by popular folk singers. If possible, obtain a recording and play the song for your class. When children are familiar with the melody, invite them to sing along with the music.

Epitaphs

Explain that an *epitaph* is an inscription on a tombstone that tells about the person buried there. Epitaphs commemorate and epitomize the dead person, and are sometimes funny or witty as well. Share the following epitaph with the class.

This is the grave of Mike O'Day
Who died maintaining his right of way.
His right was clear, his will was strong,
But he's just as dead as if he'd been wrong.

Explain that epitaphs are a very old form of poetry. They have been found on ancient Egyptian coffins. A walk through a cemetery will also reveal epitaphs. Point out that epitaphs are short, presumably because gravestones are not very big, and that epitaphs usually rhyme.

Distribute drawing paper and crayons to each child. Explain that they are to draw and cut out a tombstone for the old woman in the poem you read with them. Then have them write an epitaph on the "stone." Invite children to share their finished work with the class.

Featuring Creatures

Name _____ Date _____

Ads to Aid the Endangered

When Christina Rossetti wrote the poem "Hurt No Living Thing" in the 1800s, she had no way of knowing that her words about protecting animals would mean so much to people today. But now that so many species are endangered, her words are especially meaningful.

Hurt No Living Thing

Hurt no living thing:
    Ladybird, nor butterfly
Nor moth with dusty wing,
    Nor cricket chirping cheerily,
Nor grasshopper so light of leap,
    Nor dancing gnat, or beetle flat,
Nor harmless worms that creep.

On the lines below, try writing your own advertisement poem to make people aware that all animals need our protection. You may wish to make a colorful, eye-catching poster and write your poem on it.

_____

_____

_____

_____

_____

_____

_____

_____

_____

Featuring Creatures

Name _____ Date _____

Portmanteau Words

In each suitcase, write two or three words that could be "packed" tightly together to make a nonsense portmanteau word. Write the portmanteau word on the line below the suitcase.

Use some of your portmanteau words to create a nonsense poem about a real or imaginary creature.

_____

_____

_____

_____

_____

_____

_____

Featuring Creatures

Name _____ Date _____

Surprising Similes, Magical Metaphors

A simile is a comparison of two different things. Similes contain the words *like* or *as.* Use the pictures on each side to help you write similes, or make up your own.

_____ like _____

_____ as _____

_____

A metaphor is a direct comparison where one thing is said to *be* another. Use the pictures on each side to help you write metaphors, or make up your own.

_____ is _____

_____ is _____

_____

Use some of these similes and metaphors or write new ones and include them in a poem about animals.

Earth, Sea, & Sky

Nature in its myriad forms is the central theme of this unit. Children will feel the wind in their faces as they read "Who Has Seen the Wind?" and laugh at the characters of the Wind and the Moon as Wind tries in vain to blow Moon out of the night sky. Their senses will be awakened by Langston Hughes's "April Rain Song" and other poems about rain, sun, clouds, and snow. Since nature is the dominant theme for several forms of Japanese poetry, children will have the opportunity to write their own haiku, tanka, renga, and lanternes.

Nature's precious resources and beautiful ornaments are the subjects of several poems in "Earth, Sea, & Sky." The sea and its many treasures are the subjects of "Treasures" and "The Coral Grove." After enjoying these, readers will have opportunities to create an undersea collage and write diamantes about the ocean. Other poems will invite children to think about all of the useful products we get from trees and to contemplate what everyone can do to conserve the resources of our earth.

Where to Find More Poems

Adoff, Arnold. **Greens.** Lothrop, Lee & Shepard, 1988.

Greenfield, Eloise. **Under the Sunday Tree.** Harper, 1988.

Livingston, Myra Cohn. **Space Songs.** Holiday House, 1988.

Merriam, Eve. **A Sky Full of Poems.** Dell, 1986.

Prelutsky, Jack. **It's Snowing! It's Snowing!** Greenwillow, 1984.

Earth, Sea, & Sky

The Wind and the Moon

Said the Wind to the Moon, "I will blow
  you out;
      You stare
      In the air
    Like a ghost in a chair,
Always looking what I am about;
I hate to be watched; I will blow you out."

The Wind blew hard, and out went the Moon.
      So, deep
      On a heap
    Of clouds to sleep,
Down lay the Wind, and slumbered soon—
Muttering low, "I've done for that Moon."

He turned in his bed; she was there again!
      On high,
      In the sky,
    With her one ghost eye,
The Moon shone white and alive and plain,
Said the Wind, "I will blow you out again."

The Wind blew hard, and the Moon grew dim,
      "With my sledge
      And my wedge
    I have knocked off her edge!
If only I blow right fierce and grim,
The creature will soon be dimmer than dim."

He blew and he blew, and she thinned to a thread.
      "One puff
      More's enough
    To blow her to snuff!
One good puff more where the last was bred,
And glimmer, glimmer, glum will go
      that thread!"

He blew a great blast and the thread was gone.
      In the air
      Nowhere
    Was a moonbeam bare;
Far-off and harmless the shy stars shone;
Sure and certain the Moon was gone!

The Wind he took to his revels once more;
      On down,
      In town,
    Like a merry-mad clown,
He leaped and hallooed with whistle and
  roar—
"What's that?" The glimmering thread
  once more!

He flew in a rage; he danced and blew;
      But in vain
      Was the pain
    Of his bursting brain;
For still the broader the Moon-scrap grew
The broader he swelled his big cheeks and blew.

Slowly she grew, till she filled the night,
      And shone
      On her throne
    In the sky alone,
A matchless, wonderful, silvery light,
Radiant and lovely, the Queen of the night.

Said the Wind, "What a marvel of power am I!
      With my breath,
      Good faith,
    I blew her to death—
First blew her away right out of the sky—
Then blew her right in; what strength have I!"

But the Moon she knew nothing about the affair;
      For high
      In the sky,
    With her one white eye,
Motionless, miles above the air,
She had never heard the great Wind blare.

George MacDonald

Earth, Sea, & Sky

POEMS ON THE WIND

Who Has Seen the Wind?

Who has seen the wind?
    Neither I nor you:
But when the leaves hang trembling,
    The wind is passing through.

Who has seen the wind?
    Neither you nor I:
But when the trees bow down their heads,
    The wind is passing by.

Christina Rossetti

One March Day

As I went walking, one March day,
    Down the length of Blossom Street,
Round me whirled a wind at play,
    And lifted me right off my feet.

English Rhyme

A Kite

I often sit and wish that I
Could be a kite up in the sky,
And ride upon the breeze and go
Whichever way I chanced to blow.
Then I could look beyond the town,
And see the river winding down,
And follow all the ships that sail
Like me before the merry gale,
Until at last with them I came
To some place with a foreign name.

Frank Dempster Sherman

Kite Days

A kite, a sky, and a good firm breeze,
And acres of ground away from trees,
And one hundred yards of clean,
    strong string
Oh boy, Oh boy! I call that spring!

Mark Sawyer

Little Wind

Little wind, blow on the hilltop,
Little wind, blow on the plain,
Little wind, blow up the sunshine,
Little wind, blow off the rain.

Anonymous

Windy Nights

Whenever the moon and stars are set,
    Whenever the wind is high,
All night long in the dark and wet,
    A man goes riding by.
Late in the night when the fires are out,
    Why does he gallop and gallop about?

Whenever the trees are crying aloud,
    And ships are tossed at sea,
By, on the highway, low and loud,
    By at the gallop goes he;
By at the gallop he goes, and then
    By he comes back at the gallop again.

Robert Louis Stevenson

Wind Watching

Open a discussion with children about the wind. Encourage them to tell how they know the wind is there even though they cannot see it. Invite them to share experiences they have had with the wind, both positive and negative. Next, to produce wind, set up a small electric fan that has a protective grill. Volunteers can hold objects such as paper streamers, a paper bag, a plastic bag, feathers, and so on, in front of the fan to see what the wind does to them. Then give children heavy objects such as a big book, a rock, a chair, and so on, so they can see how these things are *not* blown. Allow volunteers to stand in front of the fan so they can see how it feels to have the wind in their faces. Turn off the fan so children can experience the calm. If the fan has several speeds, encourage children to feel the differences between high winds and gentle breezes.

Mr. Wind and Ms. Moon

After reading aloud "The Wind and the Moon," invite children to comment about what the wind tried to do and how the moon felt about it. Point out that in this poem, the wind and the moon are *personified*—they are given human characteristics. Encourage them to explain what was actually happening to the moon when it disappeared and reappeared. Several children can each read a stanza of the poem aloud. Your class might also enjoy dramatizing the poem in small groups.

Catch the Wind

Invite children to listen to what various poets think about the wind as you read aloud the poems on page 81. Invite listeners to comment on the poets' various views. Then have them share feelings about being outside on a windy day. Encourage them to think about some of the things they would not be able to do without the wind, such as sailing boats and flying kites.

Earth, Sea, & Sky

Go Fly a Kite!

Distribute two large sheets of mural or butcher paper to each child. (Give them rectangles that are approximately three times longer than they are wide.) Explain to children that they are going to make fish kites similar to the kind flown by Japanese children during special festivals. With crayons, have children draw a large fish shape on one sheet of paper. Then, holding both pieces of paper together, have them cut out the fish so they have two shapes. Children can decorate the outsides of the fish. Next, have them paste the two halves of the fish together (color sides out). Caution them to spread paste only along the outline of the fish's body, leaving the center and the sections around the mouth and tail free. Distribute a small piece of bendable wire or a pipe cleaner to each child. Instruct children to fold the wire into a hoop to fit inside the unglued mouth of the fish. Have them tape the hoop in place. The hoop will hold the fish's mouth open so the wind can blow through the center and out through the tail. Give each child two strings to fasten to both sides of the hoop. Have children knot the strings and then tie them to a ball of kite string. When the kites are finished, take your class outdoors on the next breezy day and go fly a kite!

Haiku

Haiku is a form of poetry created by the Japanese many hundreds of years ago. Print the following haiku on the chalkboard.

> Wind blowing fiercely!
> Everything whirls in its path.
> My kite dips and soars.

Read the poem aloud. Point out that most haiku are about various aspects of nature. The first and third lines in a haiku are always five syllables. The second line has seven syllables. Invite children to read the poem aloud in unison and clap out the syllables in each line.

Writing Haiku

Children can write their own haiku. You may wish to suggest that they recall their experiences with wind and flying kites and use them as the subject for their first haiku. When they have finished, encourage volunteers to share their work with the class.

Autumn Fancies

The maple is a dainty maid,
    The pet of all the wood,
Who lights the dusky forest glade
    With scarlet cloak and hood.

The elm a lovely lady is,
    In shimmering robes of gold,
That catch the sunlight when she moves,
    And glisten, fold on fold.

The sumac is a gypsy queen,
    Who flaunts in crimson dressed,
And wild along the roadside runs,
    Red blossoms in her breast.

And towering high above the wood,
    All in his purple cloak,
A monarch in his splendor is
    The proud and princely oak.

Anonymous

What Do We Plant?

What do we plant when we plant the tree?
We plant the ship, which will cross the sea.
We plant the mast to carry the sails;
We plant the planks to withstand the gales—
The keel, the keelson, and beam and knee;
We plant the ship when we plant the tree.

What do we plant when we plant the tree?
We plant the houses for you and me.
We plant the rafters, the shingles, the floors,
We plant the studding, the lath, the doors,
The beams and siding, all parts that be;
We plant the house when we plant the tree.

What do we plant when we plant the tree?
A thousand things that we daily see;
We plant the spire that out-towers the crag,
We plant the staff for our country's flag,
We plant the shade, from the hot sun free;
We plant all these when we plant the tree.

Henry Abbey

Tree Seeing

Explain to children that you are going to read a poem about trees during autumn. Invite them to picture how each type of tree looks as you read aloud "Autumn Fancies" on page 84. When children are familiar with the rhythm and rhyme schemes, invite them to read the poem aloud. Divide the class into small groups and ask each group to read a stanza.

Tell children to close their eyes and picture a tree. Encourage them to "see" the tree in vivid detail. Suggest that they think about a specific season of the year, the size of the tree, the shape of its leaves, and what animals make their homes in the tree. Ask children to open their eyes and describe in as much detail as possible the kind of tree they visualized.

Next, encourage them to make a picture of the tree they envisioned. Distribute paper and crayons or paints. Children can add a sign—or even a one-stanza poem—that tells the name of the tree and what season it is "dressed" for.

Uses of Trees

As you read "What Do We Plant?" children can think about some of the reasons why trees are so useful and important. After reading the poem, ask them to imagine what a world without trees might be like.

Tanka

Recall with children the special features of haiku. Explain that originally, haiku was used to start a longer poem called a *tanka*. The tanka gives a more complete idea of the poet's feelings by adding two more lines of seven syllables each. Like haiku, tanka are usually about nature. Read aloud this example:

Cherry blossoms swirl
From boughs heavily laden.
Summer creeps closer.

Rich red cherries will appear
When the snow petals have gone.

Invite children to write their own tanka. You might suggest that they use as a subject their pictures of autumn trees, their observances on a nature walk, or the many uses of trees.

Earth, Sea, & Sky

POEMS THAT TELL THE WEATHER

April Rain Song

Let the rain kiss you.
Let the rain beat upon your head with silver
    liquid drops.
Let the rain sing you a lullaby.

The rain makes still pools on the sidewalk.
The rain makes running pools in the gutter.
The rain plays a little sleep-song on our roof at
    night—

And I love the rain.

Langston Hughes

Raindrops

Softly the rain goes pitter-patter,
Softly the rain comes falling down.
Hark to the people who hurry by;
Raindrops are footsteps from out the sky!
Softly the rain goes pitter-patter,
Softly the rain comes falling down.

Anonymous

The Sun

The sun
Is like a big
Golden eye in the sky.
This mammoth eye, guarding the earth
Is life.

Jodelle Hulse

Earth, Sea, & Sky

The Snowman

Once there was a snowman
  Stood outside the door
Thought he'd like to come inside
  And run around the floor;
Thought he'd like to warm himself
  By the firelight red;
Thought he'd like to climb up
  On that big white bed.
So he called the North Wind, "Help me now, I pray.
  I'm completely frozen, standing here all day."
So the North Wind came along and blew him in the door,
  And now there's nothing left of him
But a puddle on the floor!

Anonymous

Silence in Camp

Today is cold;
The snow is falling.
The only noise
Is a pheasant calling.

Sioux Indian children

The Voice of Thunder

The voice of thunder
Within the dark cloud,
Again and again it sounds,
The voice that beautifies the land.

Navajo Indian

Weather

Whether the weather be fine
Or whether the weather be not,
Whether the weather be cold
Or whether the weather be hot,
We'll weather the weather
Whatever the weather,
Whether we like it or not.

Anonymous

Clouds

White sheep, white sheep
On a blue hill,
When the wind stops
You all stand still.
When the wind blows
You walk away slow.
White sheep, white sheep,
Where do you go?

Christina Rossetti

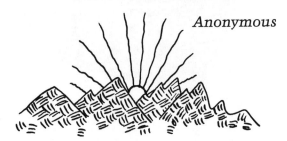

Whatever the Weather

Begin a discussion about different kinds of weather by asking children what they like to do on rainy, sunny, stormy, and snowy days. Read some or all of the weather poems on pages 86–87 and encourage listeners to compare their thoughts and feelings about the weather with the poets'.

Weather Mural

Let the class form small groups according to their favorite kinds of weather. Give each group a large sheet of mural paper and a variety of art materials such as paints, crayons, paste, foil, decorated paper, construction paper, fabric scraps, cotton balls, and popsicle sticks. Each group can make a mural depicting their favorite kind of weather. When the murals are complete, invite each group to create a poem that expresses their thoughts and feelings about weather. Have the groups display their murals and read their poems aloud to the class.

Snowy Scenes

Distribute white paint, a sheet of black construction paper, and a sheet of white drawing paper to each child. Cut up several large sponges so each student has a small piece. Invite children to make snow sponge paintings. Then have them draw, cut out, and paste paper snow figures on the black background to complete the scene.

Renga

A *renga* is made up of several tanka on the same theme. It is usually about an aspect of nature, and written by a group of people. Invite children to work in groups to write renga. One child could write the starting haiku; another, two lines that complete the first tanka; a third, another haiku keeping to the same theme; and so on.

Weather People

Assemble an assortment of art materials and invite students to design and create weather people. Suggest that in addition to more traditional snow figures, children use their imaginations to create rain people, sun people, fog people, shadow people, and so on. Children can even create puppets of the "people" they create, and have their puppets act out what the weather elements do in nature.

Lanterne

Draw the following lantern shape on the chalkboard.

Explain to children that a lanterne contains five lines arranged in the general shape of a Japanese lantern. Each line has a specified number of syllables.

Line	Syllables	Shape
1	1	—
2	2	— —
3	3	— — —
4	4	— — — —
5	1	—

You may wish to use the following lanterne to illustrate the technique and then have children write their own lanternes.

Snow
gently
falling down
white, fluffy flakes
drop.

Earth, Sea, & Sky

The Coral Grove

Deep in the wave is a coral grove,
Where the purple mullet and gold-fish rove;
Where the sea-flower spreads its leaves of blue
That never are wet with falling dew,
But in bright and changeful beauty shine
Far down in the green and glassy brine.
The floor is of sand, like the mountain drift,
And the pearl-shells spangle the flinty snow;
From coral rocks the sea-plants lift
Their boughs, where the tides and billows flow;
The water is calm and still below,
For the winds and waves are absent there,
And the sands are bright as the stars that glow
In the motionless fields of upper air.

There, with its waving blade of green,
The sea-flag streams through the silent water,
And the crimson leaf of the dulse is seen
To blush, like a banner bathed in slaughter.
There, with a light and easy motion,
The fan-coral sweeps through the clear, deep sea;
And the yellow and scarlet tufts of ocean
Are bending like corn on the upland lea.
And life, in rare and beautiful forms,
Is sporting amid those bowers of stone,
And is safe, when the wrathful spirit of storms
Has made the top of the wave his own.
And when the ship from his fury flies,
Where the myriad voices of ocean roar,
When the wind-god frowns in the murky skies,
And demons are waiting the wreck on shore;
Then, far below, in the peaceful sea,
The purple mullet and gold-fish rove
Where the waters murmur tranquilly,
Through the bending twigs of the coral grove.

James Gates Percival

Earth, Sea, & Sky

Treasures

Down on the beach when the tide is out
Beautiful things lie all about—
Rubies and diamonds and shells and pearls,
Starfish, oysters, and mermaids' curls;
Slabs of black marble cut in the sand,
Veined and smoothed and polished by hand;
And whipped-up foam that I think must be
What mermen use for cream in tea.
These and a million treasures I know
Strew the beach when the tide is low—
But very few people seem to care
For gems scattered everywhere.
Lots of these jewels I hide away
In an old box I found one day
And if a beggar asks me for bread
I will give him diamonds instead.

Mary Dixon Thayer

I Saw a Ship A-Sailing

I saw a ship a-sailing,
  A-sailing on the sea,
And, oh! it was all laden
  With pretty things for thee!

There were raisins in the cabin,
  And apples in the hold;
The sails were made of silk,
  And the masts were made of gold.

The four-and-twenty sailors
  That stood between the decks,
Were four-and-twenty white mice
  With chains about their necks.

The captain was a duck,
  With a packet on his back;
When the ship began to sail,
  The captain cried, "Quack! Quack!"

Mother Goose

Earth, Sea, & Sky

Under the Sea

Invite children to share any experiences they have had with the sea, such as swimming at the beach, riding in a boat, sailing, and so on. Read the sea poems on pages 90–91 and ask listeners to comment on how the poets view the ocean and the objects that can be found in the sea and on the shore.

Sea Treasures

Let children read "Treasures" aloud with you. Encourage them to speculate about what objects the poet might consider to be rubies, diamonds, and pearls. Provide a variety of art materials including a large sheet of lightweight cardboard, construction paper of several colors, paste, scissors, foil, and sand. Invite children to make a sea collage that shows some of the things they might find on the beach that they would consider treasures. Then have them spread a thin layer of paste on their work and sprinkle sand over it.

Diamante

Explain to your class that a diamante is a poem in the shape of a diamond. There are seven lines in a diamante with rules governing each line.

Line   Requirements
1   one-word subject: noun, opposite of word in last line
2   two words: adjectives describing subject in line 1
3   three words: participles: *-ing, -ed* words about subject in line 1
4   four words: two nouns about subject in first line and two about subject in last line
5   three words: participles: *-ing, -ed* words about subject in last line
6   two words: adjectives describing the subject in the last line
7   one-word subject: noun, opposite of word in first line

Encourage children to use this model for writing their own diamantes:

sea
brilliant, blue
swirling, tossing, lapping
whales, shells, birds, sunshine
caressing, lifting, flying
vast, endless
sky

Earth, Sea, & Sky

The Green Grass Grows All Around

Sing the first verse of "The Green Grass Grows All Around" with children. Invite them to sing the remaining verses with you. Then encourage children to continue the story by creating additional verses that could be sung to the same melody.

1. There was a tree (There was a tree) All in the wood (All in the wood),
2. Now, on that tree (Now on that tree) There was a trunk (There was a trunk),

The pret-tiest lit-tle tree (The pret-tiest lit-tle tree)
The pret-tiest lit-tle trunk (The pret-tiest lit-tle trunk)

That you ev-er did see (That you ev-er did see).
That you ev-er did see (That you ev-er did see).

Verse 2 and end of other verses   *Verse 1*   *Chorus*

Oh, the trunk on the tree and the tree in the wood, And the

green grass grows all a-round, all a-round, And the green grass grows all a-round.

3.
Now, on that trunk (Now, on that trunk)
There was a limb (There was a limb),
The prettiest little limb (The prettiest little limb)
That you ever did see (That you ever did see).
Oh, the limb on the trunk
  and the trunk on the tree
  and the tree in the wood

Chorus   And the green grass grows all around, all around,
And the green grass grows all around.

4.
Now, on that limb (Now, on that limb)
There was a branch (there was a branch),
The prettiest little branch (The prettiest little branch)
That you ever did see (That you ever did see).
Oh, the branch on the limb
  and the limb on the trunk
  and the trunk on the tree
  and the tree in the wood   *Chorus*

Earth, Sea, & Sky

Name _____ Date _____

Ecology-Minded

Although the following poem was written long ago, it tells about something with which many people today agree.

Woodman, Spare That Tree
Woodman, spare that tree!
Touch not a single bough!
In youth, it sheltered me,
And I'll protect it now.
George Pope Morris

On the lines below, try writing your own poem about something in nature that you feel should be protected. It can be a plant, an animal, or some other part of the environment.

_____

_____

_____

_____

_____

_____

_____

_____

_____

_____

_____

_____